The Hidden Chronicles

Unleashed

Poetry by

SLJ TILLMON

Dorrance Publishing Co
585 Alpha Drive
Pittsburgh, PA 15238
Visit our website at www.dorrancebookstore.com

ISBN: 978-1-6442-6174-3
eISBN: 978-1-6442-6266-5

Dear secrets

My life like yours has creases

My wounds too need stitches

A purpose finding has glitches

But a travel through the woods

A walk that became stood

All the trees looked the same

But out, my mind's journey it became

-S L J Tillmon

DEDICATED TO YOU

BROKEN

The water falls in secret
Down the curves of a face
Lists her down, soon to be erased
Useless to have cared so much
Unnoticed, a ghost she was
Disappeared, she felt worn
Forgotten, a while she was torn
A fragment of her was boiling mad
Though abandoned, tried she had
Though you left her a little broken
She moves forward deemed unchosen

BRUISED

She grieves
Her wants
Always can't have
Yet knows she's lost
Her mind unclear, her heart is fragile
Her tears become blood
A maze she travels
Roams behind walls
Not allowed where trust falls
Inside she tumbles, outside looks stable
Misunderstood and goes unlabeled
One of a kind, no one familiar
Remains bruised till she finds a healer

THE DARK

Constantly hears you
But hardly speaks
She never hurt you
In depth she believed
A support system that failed to stand
Came crashing down in the soil's hands
Peeking around she was seeing blue
Ripped her to pieces, providing no glue
The burning light flickered,
but nothing she found
Was left in the dark, and her
light inside drowned

CHILD

Cotton candy clouds
Overalls, toys, and sounds
The playground, the freedom
Free spirit, judged by no one
But then you grow up
No bubble gum or fun
Insecure, and lose sight of yourself as one
Once a child, a form we held
We keep a drop, but lose the rest itself

MAD

You killed her, you shot her down
Now she's gone mad, now roams around
Hidden away, she has run off
Hoping for regret, despising the plots
Tied up quiet, screaming her thoughts
Looks perfect as though she's got it all
Bandages to patch your sad aesthetic
Pathetic, overdosed she gets a headache
When you see her again, you confess
But by then she will have gotten someone else
Too late, so sad, leaves you feeling bad
Unmedicated you've become just as mad

I

Can be so quiet you can hear a pin drop
Parts from assemblies alike in spots
Boring is perceived, but residue is not
Noiseless secrecy does talk
Listens to advise and guide
Really bad at comforting lies
Tries to avoid confrontation and fights
Keeps the rest of her business inside
People think they know and it's fine
Shared enough so here is goodbye

RUNAWAYS

You feel crushed under their words
You feel restrained, they've done their worst
Make you feel you're never enough
Or incapable of being loved
You think it's protection through lies
But they could be truths you've cried
Tried to excuse them and got hurt
False memories, delusional turns
Let them run free then wait
The runaways come back to play
They want to be serious
They aren't as curious
When they realize they were wrong
When the past became where they belonged

MESSAGE

Leave a message after the tone
Can't pick up, though I am home
Maybe I will, maybe I won't
One missed call, ID unknown
Reserved for only who I've wrote
If important leave a note
Or do what you do best and leave me alone

RAIN

Rain, rain come and stay
Stay a while, don't go away
Help me sleep, cure the pain
A sound that pours and keeps me sane
Stay in bed, remain awake
The sun comes out and gave your name

EMPTY SOUL

A short amount of time
And you left her out to dry
And what you claimed was right
She knew it was besides
A waste of time, energy and goals
She wanted someone who wasn't cold
You needed someone to fill a hole
She needed someone who had a soul

BROKEN RECORD

Her skin becomes ice
Her body becomes thorned
Her thoughts become brittle
Her throat becomes scorned
Her heart becomes shelved
Then she collects herself
She becomes a broken record
That repeats the words that left her

ABANDONED

Contributed to your loneliness
A penny for your troubles
A brief cold heart for occasions
Some blow offs to be subtle
Now me, now me
A cut off as I received
A fuck you for the deceit
Drawing blanks when there is ink
And no ears for when you speak

GIVEN UP

I could tell you many things I know
What I know about you, who I am up close
You see I can tell you things you can't tell me
One chance, not two not even three
A loner always misunderstood
A shell that shelters until gone for good
Think I've been pushed away enough
Stitched up where the wounds are tough
And that is why I turned to stone
A reason I'd almost given up

THE CRIES

It is crazy how your organ will give out
Outlets to that one you sought around
Thrown down and your chest just bursts
Forever nothing but overworked
Still wonder, the head wanders away
Believing so many are just the same
No longer waiting, just moving on
Hoping that time when you're gone
Those find someone with open eyes
So the closed ones can hear the cries
Of the ones they split and left behind

I DON'T

The face is gone
Remembering vanished
The bull has stopped
The healing established
We just learn to ignore it
We learn to forget
The hard forgets are forgotten
To them you're hardly existent
No benefits means no relationship
In a bind means no time for it
No time for it, means not wanting to try
And don't try, the clocks unwind
I will, turns into I won't
No talking turns into we don't
And the chances of you caring after, ask them if they do
I don't and now I can't, I could but not for you

APOLOGETIC

Those eyes with sorrow
Those eyes filled with sadness
For letting go of that one thing
That stayed when you hadn't
Every day was a panic
Every day sat and waited
Emotions beat them senseless
Had nothing left, they were reckless
Eyes turned cold
Not apologetic
But the end had to be the test
They felt content with their mess

CORPSE

Underground in another zone
Skin crawling as she felt disposed
Thicker skin from all the cuts and blows
Bruises from the raw fibs they told
Buried alive but up again she rose
Sewed herself back up, it's all she knows
Now is numb and feeling gross
Walks with the world under her nose
Ends up hoping they're all alone
Dirt in her face she fell and broke
Marinates in it, now it's her home
Say to live a little, life says no
No life when life's taken, felt exposed
Her hole, she goes back for she is just a corpse
Better to party in a grave of souls
Over the life of overrated jokes

INVISIBLE

The little misfit
Why do I exist?
A world full of shit
And the people so sick
But I'm not here
I've disappeared
In the mirror, yet to appear
Closer than I actually am
And as silent as the lambs
Judgment louder than your grand
I'm transparent sometimes
Feel so lost in these lives
I've been hit, passed through the side
But I can see, they can see
Few people see me, I believe
Loyalty stands but the fakes they rather please
So I shut the doors and windows
Erase my visibility

F#@* OFF

Got swayed in the worst way
Shut down on the worst day
Fired from the latest flame
Ignored, implied to go away
Put on hold and left, wait
Stabbed with the sharp blades
Heard the no you can'ts
Slapped with the dumbest rants
Tasted losing, the taste was bland
And I've felt appalled
It rubs you fairly wrong
It made me stronger through it all
When I say I don't care about how you are
Said truthfully, not your call
And yes hello, I cared, excuse me and fuck off

BED CRY

Her cheeks are wet
From all the stories unread
Unfinished she lays her head
Aching her life has bled
Deeply she sounds unsaid
Rainwater fills her bed
The bed cry she sleeps again
Wakes up and repeats those steps

PLAYGROUND

Ran and fell
Scraped up knee
Screams and yells
Band-aids and swings
Slides down the rails
Climbs and sings
Hides and seeks
Jumps and flings
Finders they keep
Bars they cling
Loudness they shriek
Playgrounds they bring
Reality's where we plead
For those playgrounds were only dreams

MONSTERS

The real monsters are human
The actual monsters we fear aren't real
Not in our closets, not under your bed
They are all disguised or inside our own heads
But that is only what they've said
'Cause see the monsters are always there
Whether you see them or not is fair
But don't be too sure they don't all exist
For they can be within, they're everywhere

SPOTTED BEAUTY
BEHIND THE CRACKS

The ability to understand the misunderstood
To look at the weeds and see a garden
To embrace what little would
Or connect where little could
You see where there is nothing to see
But I see behind what you've hidden from me
They see part of what you may live
I saw beyond the walls, beauty there is
I spotted beauty behind the cracks
I spotted charm, humor in paths
Severed, and severed's never the same
But I'd be the paste when you shattered again

AWFUL PERSON

Have I become this awful person?
Why does this question rise to surface?
Am I hurt and hurting others?
Am I confused, scared under covers?
Have I become a lazy person?
Have I become this worthless person?
Have I become purposeless?
Existing but no reason to, maybe in distress
I care, I do, maybe too redundant
Care too much? No, but slivered rugged
Why am I breathing, sinking?
Complicated thinking
Keep digging graves, I've stopped blinking
Crushed into one field, stuck on leaving
I'm not an awful person
I've only had things worsen
I'm rotting from this on the inside
Rotting, deserving from these hands of mine

SHUTTERS

Let the shutters shut
Let out reasons of who you've become
Keep them closed so no one hears
To yourself, let the memories pierce
Feel them stab from head to spine
Insides scream deadly cries
Remains silent outside
In you where it feeds and hides
Let the shutters open
Let out what you don't owe them
Keep them open to throw up what destroys
Already started don't avoid the noise
Let someone peek through
Can they finally interpret you?
Lie still as the body lifts from the ocean
Underneath where it had no motion

MOTIONLESS

To not be able to listen
The voice that exudes bliss
The heart stronger than it is
If one day it all stops
Blood flow will just drop
A visioned future won't knock
Caged in will be locked
Motionless and feeling lost
How devastating if you were gone
Would cry for days that feel too long
Suffocate and drown in the water I spill
It could be the very day the earth stands still

THE FLAME

A fire burns where a flame is lit
Ignites realism, its purest lives
The smoke turns black
The chemicals collapse
In another life
The same match, would light its wax
The same moon will meet the sun
The same hearts will beat as one
The same paint will find its brush
The same fear will find its trust
Eagerness when one is away
Brief lonesome till you're back to stay
Time became a gift for two
Selective conscious thoughts of you

IMPERFECT

What is imperfection?
If it's you, well then I love it
Amusing from all angles
Uniformity feels unpleasant
May not have the best blue sight
But I swim and whelm every time
Those stems that hold the beat of life
And breaths that may speed up are mine
Unstable build, but walks for miles
And your effort brings all light inside
Insecure sometimes you disguised
Sure you're not perfect, neither am I
But flawless you fit into my life

IS IT EVEN HUMAN?

Is it even humanly possible
To miss someone so much
To be so dowsed in love
To think of them all day
But for you it's all enough
Feel a tingle when distance takes
Like a fire sealed untamed
Soften at the sight of their name
To hurt when they're in pain
Only think of them may seem insane
But fills us up the best damn way
If this isn't human oh well, okay
Where humans crowd we have our cave

GOODNIGHT

The night's became the best and the worst
A friend and an enemy intertwined and conversed
If out too late no time reimbursed
A night out translates into a curse
Changes in plans just doesn't work
But we try and try, it keeps us alive
The life we live relies on time
Some days not fed leads towards a cry
You always dig for as much you can find
Push for five minutes before saying goodnight

SORRY

It wasn't expected to get no response
Had there been trauma left from loss
Where there shouldn't be war, somehow we fought
Maybe too late, but unwanted I thought
No seriousness, desires soon forgot
And leave it all behind to relieve what's not
If never interacting again, a lot in my fault
But dearly sorry, wishing your life goes on

HAPPY BIRTHDAY?

Forgive me if I am wrong
Would feel silly if all along
Your beginning isn't till tomorrow
Or days after then that follow
But a moment to confess
The cause of some distress
A checkmate to my chess
A greater to my less
A beauty who doesn't know
A flare where passion froze
An art worth 1,000 notes
And the feelings one can't dispose

MY SICKNESS

I stressed this poem for you
Perfect some weren't, so I made a few
This one might be the fourth, the best I assume
I hope that this makes your day just bloom
Some peace for all of the pieces we've glued
A kiss for the French I speak better than you
A kidding for the last line because it's untrue
But you're the depth I get lost in when I'm blue
The escape I run away, a taste I consume
A love that spreads throughout a room
It spread over to me and I caught the flu
A picture that says more than words ever do
There are not enough words to describe such proof
That gravity meshed one heart out of two

HEADACHE

A year gone by, could have gone better
Moments that could haunt me forever
Proud of some agony caused, not ever
Hoping winter lifts me from under the weather
Brief ups, exhausted coming down
Intense situations, reputations clowned
Jokes later to hold as a shield now
Sweet escapes that assisted you out
Some murky unsatisfying
Oh how the head just pounds
Gained a new perspective
On days looking from the ground

A NEW PLACE

Not every day is replete with light
Not every emotion is elated inside
Not every memory is desired in mind
And a lot envisioned, released from sight
In the new place lessons are learned
Captivated by suppressed ill curbs
Adjust your eyes in the dark you yearn
Bound in there till you aren't who you were
One day crosses you are informed
Waking up the light bulb is born
A breakthrough from gifts and signs, you're sore
A change needed to gravitate from mourn

NUMB

The silence can be a call for help
A depressed, critical version of self
Reflections loud and poke at your health
Eyes shut to repress truths and lies you sell
A single hello, knocks you out of trance
A face, a smile that gives you a chance
A fix where one breaks lends a hand
The numbness cured and self worth stands
The finder keeps one on their feet
The keeper finds themselves a key
The beautiful mess was lost and found
Eludes to a numb she wants around

HAUNTED

Paranoia shadowing you, it stalks
Do it, don't, you're tough, you're soft
Left, right, back forward it walks
Distractions from decisions flies in flock
Some days effortless and others seek your stop
Haunted by the body you belong

PRETEND

A snooze to dream of pretend things
A cent to pretend a way of living
A game to disguise what could be real
An I don't care to hide what we feel
Pretend to pretend the truth can be rare
And it can't be handled when they're never aware

BREATHLESS

Heart beating its fastest pace
A touch ruptures the lungs out of place
Transformed spread from their cocoon
Presents themselves as your next move
Relentlessly gasping for air
Unreal, relieved that you are there
Amusing you are, she smiles wide
Leaves her breathless every time

A PUPPET

Can't manage yourself
Can't control your health
That mini ego melts
Wearing it right on your belt
Your strings go up
Your senses wouldn't shut
It's your master want to run
But attached you feel you're done
Let the curtains open
Heard the laughs awoken
They paid only in tokens
Breaking down, words unspoken
One day you're hanging in
Free the ropes from each limb
Balance and walk you begin
Be the puppeteer you wished

I'M OKAY

I'm okay, I am fine, I am good
Such a liar
I am cool, I am calm, I am strong
Close to a cipher
You're okay, you'll be fine, you belong
And I meant it
Such a shame, it's a test, am I wrong?
Too far from selfish
I have to be okay, you have to be okay
If you scream, I have to touch the flames
Becomes difficult when you feel the same
But I can't be in the dark when your sky is grey
And I say it, even untrue, I'm okay

STUPID

No one is fluent in confusion
Examine all involved emotion
Too many hearts, you don't want frozen
Too many words, limits you spoke them
No more fence, unshielded road
Like learning to walk, but to you it's unknown
Riding a bike, fall as you're let go
Brace for the landing, hurts but you grow
And sometimes you'll look stupid
But at least now you know

ALONE

The urge to turn off my connection
I'm returning to sulk in reflection
Dismissed just stare at the message
Losing all affection arrested
Maybe this is why I never did this
Maybe I'm just no good and should quit
Maybe I'm really just full of shit
Maybe I don't deserve what I give
I'm tired, I'm stressing, I'm dim
Pitch black I talk to my tears and they win
Remember everything you had did
Thought you were healing, you are sick
You lay in silence on hold
Thinking loudly on your own
You realize again you fell apart
And soon might be that all alone

FOUR IN ONE

Once there was one
Story time begun
Then there were two
Unsure who is who
Then there were three
Stand far back to see
Close up there were four
Inside I closed the door
Open I grew sore
Peeking I cared to warm
An invitation in
Where the same story lived

JOKE'S ON ME

So the joke is on me
Ha ha the tricks lie free
Jack in the box, don't know who to believe
May be a cruel surprise, how sweet
Stop playing now, its tiring to feed
And it's real on my side, I need
The magic show to disappear, to leave

INTROVERSION

Tick-Tock

Is all I hear when the noise stops

Internally loud hearing my own thoughts

Sleepless, insomnia clots

So cloudy and foggy up top

Head thuds

Can't recall how to have fun

I'm not like them, table for one

The world just doesn't get us

They think we're boring, sucks huh?

We aren't them

We don't fit in

I'm not like him

I'm not who she is

Just a nonconformist

INHIBITED

I'm no model
No Victoria Secret on the TV screen
Not the rack and the back or so to speak
Don't always like what I'm made to see
Wondering what they think about me
But we all have insecurities
Check for flaws in the morning
Gain a pound and you're pouring
You're okay, not tall enough
Way too small, doesn't talk much
If they only knew who she was
They would know she's more than said above

HIDE AND GO SEEK

Ending nights in wordless fights
Silence becomes our biggest pry
Pillows qualify as shoulder cries
Under the sheets where we go hide
Realizations tell us it's fine
Come out and open arms are kind
Rub off damage, closest to mine
Long hellos and brief goodbyes

EARTH

The earth from the outside
The reality so far behind
The moon to take your fears
The wind listens, becomes your ears
The garden grows all of your tears
Those tears create the river you're near
And you can't swim, but drift to your pier
All beauty you desire resides here

DESTRUCTION

I don't know what's wrong
Always tired, can't nod it off
That cursive sensation I don't belong
Hunger, starving, weakened I crawl
No longer standing, legs fail, I fall
Dragging, held up the bricks for so long
Stand one last time and be strong
If trouble comes, we destroy till it's gone

SPIRITS

All we believed in
All that we've wanted
Lies they hid in our closets
Little girl don't believe them
They won't let your spirits in
They think you're easy to miss
That your darkness is your only bliss
Try to repair a light they don't need to fix
That their teachings you should be with
You're the only you that you've wished
Given the only dream you can finish

THE ORGAN

The melody
Haunted it seems
But plays such beauty
Whispers words fluently
Concentration thought loosely
But the heart of that moves me

LONER

So I'm the loner, maybe you're right
But at least I have a friend in line
Don't need a million seasonal times
So you thought, smirk your tiresome smile
Surprise, surprise who has a friend
They aren't revealed until the end
One is found and the rest will mend
Can keep on longing to blend
While the loner here looks to descend

THRESHOLD

Conservative exterior

Walks to become inferior

Skin winks to become superior

Weight riding on the borderline

Sweat off the unsatisfied

Into the threshold you designed

Let us walk out undefined

CAPTIVE

Don't let them down
Hold up your crown
Clean off the cloak in a confined town
Locked in a cage
From all mistakes
Remind you why you avoid the phase
Unlock the chains
Unleash your reins
Captive refuse to be enslaved

AMUSEMENT

Step into the show
Brace for the rides before you head home
Rigged the games, win when you're old
Sit on the coaster and up we go
Shhh, don't let them know
Scared to hit the ground a solus soul
After the ride, the smile is gold
It went well so you reply
But do not get back in line
A close call, no need to rewind
Might blow your cover next time

ROSES

Who loves me? Who loves me not?
The petals float soundly
Her stems that hold what's locked
A velvet touch surrounds herBut prickly she pricks a lot
You bleed but it's her plead
Care for her flowers not to rot
Accept all of her weeds
And water where she has gone

INNOCENCE

No blossoms blooming in spring
No bird spreading their wings
Not yet, next time little thing
It's not only in your dreams
Patience will grow the seeds
Be unafraid when two worlds meet

ROOM

The doorknob, I'm jailed in from the outside
Should be restraining but I'm not surprised
Can be so isolated and I'm unsure why
But in peace, I'm still alive
In the room of sacred mind
Knocking won't let you inside
Can't trespass this world that is mine

AWAKE

Though my eyes are closed
The subconscious remains open
The feelings unexposed
Body stays awoken
Sensitive to the emotion
Curious discoveries are potent
Not asleep through the haze
But trapped in a dream of day
Sleepwalk the moods away
Most nights aware I am awake

GHOSTS

I'm sensing some presence
Breathes my imperfections
Attempting to hear less
Escaping to keep compressed
Paralyzed, can't move ahead
A bite spreads to inflection
Hair raising from the lessons
She is not seen or mentioned
A ghost who seeps to regression

IN THE COLD

She's aging another decade
Just hoping that it won't fade
Days passing, she's craveless
Her moods are so distant
Different, missing pieces
Conscience not always keeping her warm
Not the same as when you were born
Doing less of what you're told
Cause you are buried in the cold

QUIET

Sweet silence, but dangerous
It feeds me all tales
Start asking what sane was
Judgment walks these trails
Wary it just reminds us
But in the end quiet's no fail
That peace becomes our sail

WRITER'S BLOCK

Can't come up with the next page
Struggling on what else to say
But a listener it stays that way
Just need the words to hit my brain
The lead to write exactly the same
Writer's block calls my name
Watch it slowly go away
Continue the book, prolong to create

SLEEPLESS

Tired and young
Shouldn't that start after pleasure?
Guess this life is not the one
Early birds must re-measure
Drowsy, hibernating not once
Close your bagged eyes
Pray to doze off at night
And awake with better sight

MAKE BELIEVE

I hear the train go by
So far from what's mine
In a bay window I don't have
Daydream the dreams of sacred plans
Till they are real, I see
They're only make believe
They're only dreams to me
From the ground it's just a seed

CARNIVAL

Just hanging around
Near class acts and clowns
And drama mask frowns
The happiest come out
Performing are we now?
But I got my head in the clouds
The carnival can't take me down
Play engage these towns
But I'm straying from them now

WEEPING WILLOW

Gracefully moves like the wind
Weeping beauty within
Delicate she cracks her vines
But strong enough she holds on tight
And she's one of few who knows it
Sees right through her image
Mysterious her flow is
And well aware she's different

BREATHE

This world is choking me
Can't gasp for air, lungs suffering
So much deeper than we think
So far gone we can't see a thing
Swimming until we sink
Then slowly float back up to breathe

GRAVE

Shovel into the ground
Bury the bullshit six feet down
Fill the hole with the dirt I found
In the grave, it's dead to me now
And for sure it's for the best
Maybe now give it some rest
In peace where we once met
Into the grave that it once slept

GREY CLOUDS

A storm is coming
The rain keeps falling
The birds are running
The lightening calling
The thunder's humming
They drift above me
Save me some serenity
Sometimes defining
The nights surrendering
The moon to escape free
The days of clarity
And frightening they can be
The grey clouds are half sanctuary
But I need the sun to shine between
A balance to cure me
Please

FOUR-EYED GIRL

No I was never popular
No I don't look just like her
Accuracy preferred...
One point tried to fit in
The sake of self protection
Doesn't work, still weird to them
Somehow not as pretty
With the lenses, no, really?
"Always unappeased"
Not attractive, try surgery
Try contacts, cute you'll be
Suggesting change for me
Putting on the opposite thing

CHAOS

The buildings come crashing down
Glass breaking, head is loud
Abandoned, they all stare now
Dead end, no going around
Spinning like a merry go round
Can't touch the ground
So heavy the chaos sounds

DRUGS

Need an AA meeting
An addiction I keep taking
Not shaking this feeling
The layers you itch on peeling
The dose you keep injecting
Is a cure, I'm shot accepting
Though the needle holds drugs
Don't mind a pick me up
Holds me when times are rough
Vulnerable but just enough
The only drug I've grown to love

ASHES

A wildfire that spread
Explains ashes shed
They land from the sky
And burn through long nights
Blackened our own homes
They become only coal
Rebuild all over again
Wash old ashes to past tense

GARDEN

Start as a little tree
Sprout into what is me
Grow as each season peaks
Away from immaturity
In my garden, flowers bound in
Roses redden
The walkways saving
Walls just caving
Hedges hiding what I'm shying
Barefoot I'm behaved
Lost inside a maze
Completely in touch I am afraid
In my garden should be no shame

BANDAGES

Cuts and scars we create
Split too deep, we heal late
Bruises, skin's not the same
Alcohol to ease our pain
And new people from kids
Want to revive this
Won't allow them advantages
To remove these bandages

SECOND PLACE

Second child on the
second day

Chosen first if all work
no play

But not the first pick
to a last name

See a future or a
dream you crave

First sight I'm not
the vision

Second to burn the
bridges

Problems, first to try
and fix it

But second chosen if I
messed it

All get playtime, I'm
sitting the benches

I'm keeping
it cool

Internally
overdue

Damn insecure
pool

Compliments
of brief use

All into
someone else

Can't help but
isolate myself

Deal the cards
I have been dealt

A queen of hearts
for my health

No ribbon, just
on the shelf

To settle for when
there's no one else

ANGELS

Angels whisper to me
Words I might be deflecting
Share them honestly
Signs of where I'm meant to lead
Small fine print I cannot read
Show me the path I can't see
Clear my conscience, it's smoggy
Light working viewing skies dusky
Forgot my purpose, my memory
Remind me, I'm forgetting
My angels I need recovering

CLOUDS

Desire floating over the sea
Sailing away from the disease
Boredom mixed, depressive sleep
Levitate over the clouds
They won't follow me now
Stay till it all calms down
It's not realistic, wear your gloves
Back underwater, wash the blood
Contaminated, swallow mistrust
Evaporate when you're back up
From above, scope destruction done

SERIOUSLY

Don't say much of anything
When I do let's hope after I think
Otherwise I'm being mean
Seriously? Seriously
My face expressions fail
Keep to myself, couldn't tell?
Maybe it holds me to a cell
But it holds me to the ground as well
Seriously? Seriously

TREES

What's beyond the trees?
Abroad the leafy heath?
Trapped don't want to leave
Find our way back to the stream
Losing track of our growth
But we can't, we have to go
Revisit the trees when you're done
Reach and climb, burn off your ton
Let time and patience react as one

LIES

Lies become webs
Truths become red
Not blissfully deceived
Morals can end in grief
The truth will set you free
But why do both tend to feel weak?

END OF THE TUNNEL

Squint, the light where could it be?
Walking the dark, no electricity
Eyes adjust from once unseen
Unsure where to go and be
Linger through the pathway
End of the tunnel that way
No matter the turns or moving straight
You get to where you're meant to stay

UNFORTUNATE

Unfortunate things affect the stealth
Causes me to exclude myself
Try to keep a peace of mind
Surely things eat me up inside
Buried by what I can't get right
Missteps too sorry for story time

CANDLE

Relighting the candle
A scent I bare to handle
A favorite I'm a fan so
Run out and I want more
Fills my room, ask an encore
A fire fit to blaze my torch

STORM

The thunder cracks my skull
Opens a fresh hello
Great lightning strikes the soul
Electrifies what is broke
The wheels spin on this road
And a tornado sweeps us close

REMAINS

Bones constricted
Caged in conflicted
A few wounds self inflicted
Until released with longing wishes
Be what you want to claim
Remove the old, conceal the remains
Don't look back, a past won't save
Keep the keys, but lose the chains

SOLITUDE

Seclusion is the solution for lucidity
Quiet down the loudness doesn't know me
Close your ears and silence starts to reek
The racket inner voices screech
Erase and rewrite your inner peace
Sanction solitude to iron your crease

GLOOMY

The sun's out but I'm worrisome
Want to leave but I haven't much
The credit is killing me, I'm glum
But I shouldn't be under pounds
Sometimes I need to settle down
Too young to ride on doubts
I'll make it where I'm meant to be
Right now sitting gloomy
Helpful this time polluted me

TICKET

Bought a ticket to the saddest show
Smiles for the audience, weeps on her pillow
Hard when prone to feeling alone
When progress is the same place don't gloat
Nothing funny when you're stuck afloat
Sea sick, continue to move the boat
Realize you're just ill from being broke
Applaud for her when she's finally home

SENSITIVE

Why are you crying?
Asked like I'm defying
My nature is my own
My low voice is my tone
I can't scream much louder
Mistaken the founder
Can't read the poker face
Somehow skim it fast pace
Sensitive and fragile
The bullet proof shell fractures

LOST AND FOUND

She's missing, oh where did she go?
She's missing, searching on her own
The journey seems eternal but glows
Obstacles will dim the light, she slows
Hunts for what she's lost for now
Depressed in the fog that surrounds
Drags forward for clarity and ground
Hope what's missing is lost and found

HYPNOSIS

Mind is spinning in another realm
Twisted, looping underneath a spell
Sentiment insists I might need help
If under hypnosis, don't lose yourself
Defeat the curse, not who you've felt

CLOSED BOOK

The pages aren't for everyone
Cover to cover, weighs a ton
Hopes her book is a better one
Filled with beauty and lots of love
A closed book she starts untouched
But the reader who stays opens her up

FEAR

Fear of rummaging
Fear of suffering
Fear of loss
Fear of thoughts
Fear of heights
Fear to fall
Fear of being unloved
Fear the world wants blood
And what is yet to come

LAUGH

I'm not always mad
I'm content or braving drafts
Not always happy where I am
But daydream a world of allure
Healthy gardens and cut grass
Clean streets, good times that last
What do you want you may ask
To succeed, to love and to laugh

PAST LIFE

I've been believing I was here once
A purpose I sense but can't touch
Close, on the tip of my tongue
My past life is calling me to the front
Have a reason but unsure what it was
Appears new but don't know what it does

IMMORTAL

Turn the lights off
Lay a while, watch the ceilings
Pray for them to come along
And live a life worth stealing
My immortal sobs aren't sleeping
Remind me why this world you keep me

RECREATION GROUND

Nobody wants to play with me
Here hanging by these strings
Think I may have lost my wings
Falling off the monkey bars, it stings
Slide down where the angel sings
Help me heal, I'm shivering
Want to fly, that's all I need
Don't want my play ship to sink
Till I'm ready I comfort the swings

LIGHTEST FEATHER

Want to land on your feet
Softly you won't hear a peep
Desire to summon my branch leaves
Each step like you weigh nothing
The lightest feather stumbling
Remove the load that's hovering

SKELETON

Hiding in your closet
The skeletons hang wantless
But they stay there solid
Forward lacking logic
Locked away as you promised

PUNISH

It's punishment enough
Know deep down you are tough
Convinced more life is rough
No need for points I do myself
Punishing more than you ever will
Don't need your hot water to melt
Or an empty glass that didn't fill

HUMMING BIRD

The light shines in the window
Eyelashes blink soft hellos
Strange soul shaking light
Sings a tune and starts to fly
A humming bird she became
Visits flowers once in her veins

TALL TALES

Thought you were joking
Turns out some truth is soaking
Those fairy tales happened to be lies
With the darkest truths hidden inside
Those tall tales in the spider web
Wrapped in a past they wanted dead
Be careful, listen to what they said
It's easy to get trapped instead

BRIDGE

Cross over to the other side
Leave and burn what torments behind
Forgive to live your best life
Watch the view over the time
Glance back and for once be fine

SOULS

Let your spirit seep out
Let it light the way
Balance your fires and bounds
Raise your soul out of its cave
Away from its harbored grave
Over the clouds through the gates

FORGOTTEN

Do you want to be a memory?
Placed behind the scenes?
So long as not forgotten
Even by just two or three
Don't want to go so lonely
Alone in my head till freed

JESTER

In the deck of cards
Sneaking away my hearts
Spades cut, ripping through
Card wearing a costume
A jester, doesn't belong here
The jokesters start to appear

SWIM

Not lost within shallow end
Swim the depths of the ocean
Hold your breath the sky watches
Pressure the lungs say stop it
They get some air and hold again
Swim the waves and conquer them

INSTRUMENT

A violin during sunrise
The harp to my soul
Sweet piano of the night
Strums the guitar to unfold
Drums that pump the chest
And the voice is very best

TRANQUILITY

Surrounded by nature's breath
The heat and the stress
Locate what seems right
Feel tranquility in nothing less
Relieve all wounds and headaches
Send all away till none is left

MOSAIC

Those shattered pieces
Pick them up and glue ceaseless
Those colors only shine through it
Puzzled to figure out the ruins
The mosaic, your grace is lucid

METAMORPHOSE

Felt so imaginary
Check for monsters out to get me
No idea what they're thinking
To reading intentions grieving
Little game of I spy
Look and see the same sights
Adult-like you brace for fights
Forget you are still a child

HOLLOW

You're more than worthless
You're just as much a person
Listening to those who follow
Only will make you hollow
Your tears have a purpose
Don't waste them on the wordless

RELEASE

Where the emotions suffer
Let it slip through your fingers
Open the door to prevent smother
Sealed into ink and a cover
Creep out once and release another
Let light in by removing clutter
Make those walls less of a mutter
Let them go and watch them flutter

LULLABY

Rest your head
Brought alive, I'm here instead
Comfort, those cheeks can't be red
How sweet unexpected
The eclipse changed our minds
Winter said goodbye
The fall said it's time
Spring shined us bright
Whistled new lullabies
And seasons that are kind

THE END

Secrets are still secrets
Sentiment did some spilling
Those assumed to know me
It's only the beginning
Maybe not the deepest
But it's hard to do I swear
Probably wait for next time
For new skin to bare

THANK YOU

Attempt to stop craze
Remove all of these blades
And keep them away
Towards less painful days
Try to keep from shame
Apologize, takes the blame
But I've turned the page
Through it all, it's okay
Attached different ways
Thank you, I feel safe

THE END